RESPIRATION AND CIRCULATION

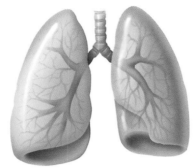

For a free color catalog describing Gareth Stevens' list of high-quality books and multimedia programs, call 1-800-542-2595 (USA) or 1-800-461-9120 (Canada). Gareth Stevens Publishing's Fax: (414) 225-0377. See our catalog, too, on the World Wide Web: gsinc.com

Library of Congress Cataloging-in-Publication Data

Llamas, Andreu.
[Respiración y la sangre. English]
Respiration and circulation / by Andreu Llamas ; illustrated by Luis Rizo.
p. cm. — (The human body)
Includes bibliographical references and index.
Summary: Describes the structures and functions of the respiratory and circulatory systems, including the lungs and airways, blood cells, the heart, arteries, veins, capillaries, pulmonary circulation, and the lymphatic system.
ISBN 0-8368-2110-6 (lib. bdg.)
1. Respiration—Juvenile literature. 2. Blood—Circulation—Juvenile literature. 3. Cardiopulmonary system— Juvenile literature. [1. Respiratory system. 2. Circulatory system.] I. Rizo, Luis, ill. II. Title. III. Series: Llamas, Andreu. The human body.
QP121.L5713   1998
612.1—dc21   98-16720

The editor would like to extend special thanks to Ronald J. Gerrits, Ph.D. (Physiology), Medical College of Wisconsin, Milwaukee, Wisconsin, for his kind and professional help with the information in this book.

First published in North America in 1998 by
Gareth Stevens Publishing
1555 North RiverCenter Drive, Suite 201
Milwaukee, WI 53212 USA

This U.S. edition © 1998 by Gareth Stevens, Inc.
Original edition © 1997 by Ediciones Lema, S. L., Barcelona, Spain.
Additional end matter © 1998 by Gareth Stevens, Inc.

U.S. series editor: Rita Reitci
Editorial assistant: Diane Laska

Printed in Mexico

1 2 3 4 5 6 7 8 9 02 01 00 99 98

Gareth Stevens Publishing
MILWAUKEE

The Nasal Fossae

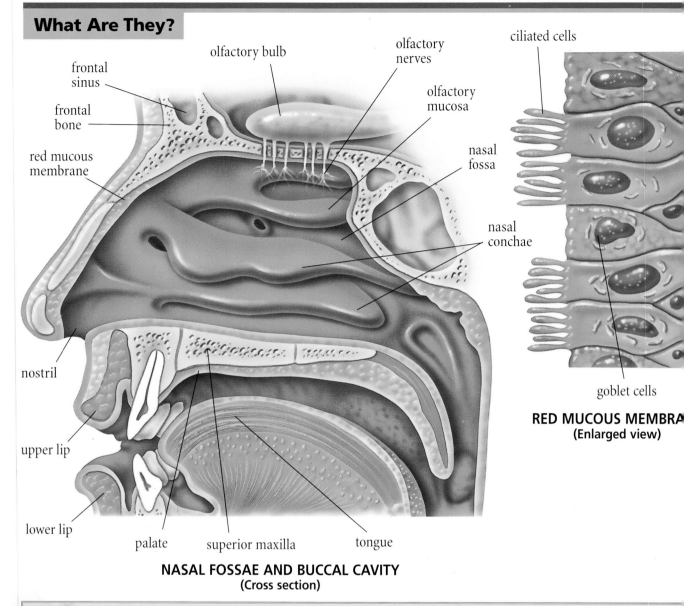

NASAL FOSSAE AND BUCCAL CAVITY
(Cross section)

RED MUCOUS MEMBRA
(Enlarged view)

Airways. The respiratory system is made up of the nose, mouth, pharynx, larynx, trachea, bronchi, and lungs. Air enters through the nose and mouth.

In addition to the mouth being necessary for processing food, it also is part of voice and speech.

The nose is made of bone and cartilage. Two nostrils form the entrance to the nasal fossae, or cavities. Hairs at the entrance to the nostrils filter the entering air.

A thin, vertical blade of cartilage, the nasal septum, separates the two fossae. Each cavity is lined with cartilage that forms three shelves, known as conchae, on its outer surface. The inside of the nose is covered with mucus. This is a fluid produced by goblet cells in a cellular layer called the red, or nasal, membrane. The red membrane also contains cells bearing cilia, which are tiny movable filaments that sweep microorganisms and small debris out of the nasal fossae.

The upper area of the mucous membrane is called the yellow mucous membrane. This is the olfactory mucosa, made up of supporting cells and spindle cells. The spindle cells project tiny hairlike structures to the membrane surface. These are the olfactory cells that detect odors.

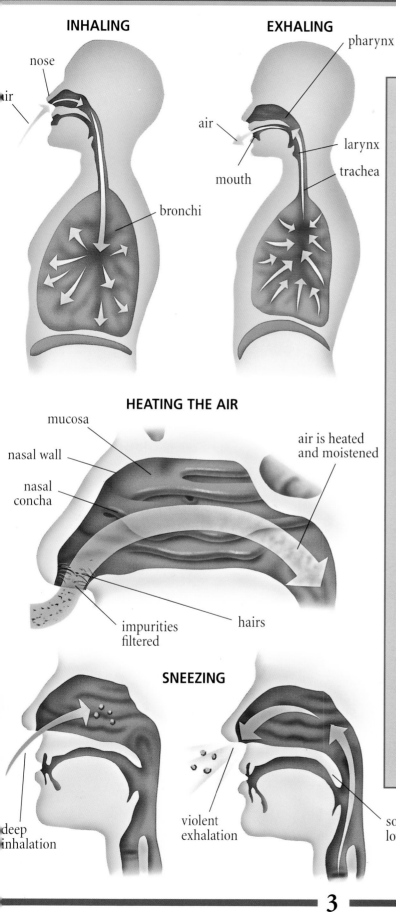

INHALING

nose

air

bronchi

EXHALING

pharynx

air

larynx

trachea

mouth

HEATING THE AIR

mucosa

nasal wall

nasal concha

air is heated
and moistened

impurities
filtered

hairs

SNEEZING

deep
inhalation

violent
exhalation

soft palate
lowers

Inhaling and exhaling. Each inhaled breath draws oxygen-rich air into the body through the nose or mouth. Air then passes through the pharynx, larynx, and trachea, and continues to travel throughout the bronchi and bronchioles of the lungs. In the blood, carbon dioxide is exchanged for the incoming oxygen. Carbon dioxide leaves the body through exhaled air.

Heating the air. When air enters the body through the nose, the nasal fossae process it. First, hairs inside the nostrils filter out dust and other particles and the pathogens they may be carrying. Secondly, the mucosa heats the air. It is able to do this because it is well supplied by blood vessels that maintain a constant temperature inside the nose. Finally, mucus secreted by the mucosa moistens the air. This prevents dry air from irritating the airways. The mucus that covers the walls of the nasal fossae also prevents infection by trapping micro-organisms. Cilia sweep the micro-organisms away. Warm, humid, and clean air then goes to the lungs.

Sneezing. Sneezing is a reflex action that is needed to clean the nose of dust and irritating particles. Sneezing takes place when air impurities inside the nasal fossae irritate the nasal mucous membranes. During a sneeze, air is violently expelled through the nose and the mouth, cleaning the fossae of infectious or irritating particles.

The Pharynx

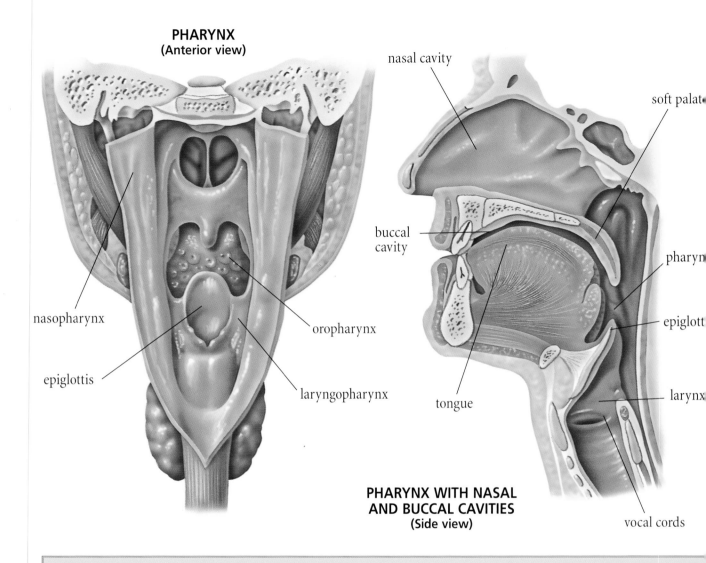

PHARYNX
(Anterior view)

nasopharynx

epiglottis

oropharynx

laryngopharynx

nasal cavity

soft palat‹

buccal
cavity

pharyn

tongue

epiglott‹

larynx

PHARYNX WITH NASAL
AND BUCCAL CAVITIES
(Side view)

vocal cords

Moving air and food. The pharynx is a muscular tube 4.7-5.5 inches (12-14 centimeters) long, located behind the nasal fossae and the buccal cavity, reaching down to the esophagus and the larynx. It is broad at the top and narrows toward the esophagus. The pharynx receives the two Eustachian tubes, each connecting the middle ear with the buccal, or mouth, cavity. The Eustachian tubes balance the air pressure on both sides of the eardrums.

The upper pharynx, which connects with the nasal fossae, is called the nasopharynx. It allows passage for air only. The oropharynx lies behind the buccal cavity. The lowest part of the pharynx, the laryngopharynx, connects with the esophagus and the larynx. These two sections allow passage of food and air, but not at the same time. Their muscles act as part of the swallowing reflex.

The epiglottis is a flap-shaped valve that separates the larynx from the pharynx. This flap closes the airway during swallowing to keep food from entering. The tonsils are two small oval bodies located on each side of the throat at the back of the mouth. Tonsils are formed from lymphatic tissue. They contain numerous white blood cells. The job of these cells is to fight off infections caused by viruses and bacteria.

ACTION OF THE PHARYNX DURING SWALLOWING

alimentary bolus

pharynx

epiglottis

larynx

alimentary bolus

Epiglottis closes access to airways

Epiglottis opens after bolus enters esophagus

Dual use. The pharynx and the larynx are part of the digestive and respiratory systems. Food goes through the pharynx as it travels toward the stomach. Air also passes through the pharynx, and then the larynx, on its way to the lungs.

The swallowing reflex. During swallowing, a series of reflex actions rapidly takes place. The tongue pushes food, in the shape of an alimentary bolus, into the pharynx. The muscles of the pharynx contract to push the bolus onward, and breathing stops. The soft palate rises to block the entry of the bolus into the nasopharynx. The larynx rises and moves forward, making room for the bolus to pass. A valve called the epiglottis shuts off the airway to the lungs so food doesn't enter to cause choking. The vocal cords contract and close the glottis, or opening of the larynx. The muscular walls of the pharynx continue pushing the bolus into the esophagus. There, waves of contractions, or peristalsis, move the food down to the stomach. Talking or laughing while eating sometimes causes particles of food to enter the airway. This causes choking and coughing in an attempt to expel the particles.

The Larynx, Vocal Cords, and Speech

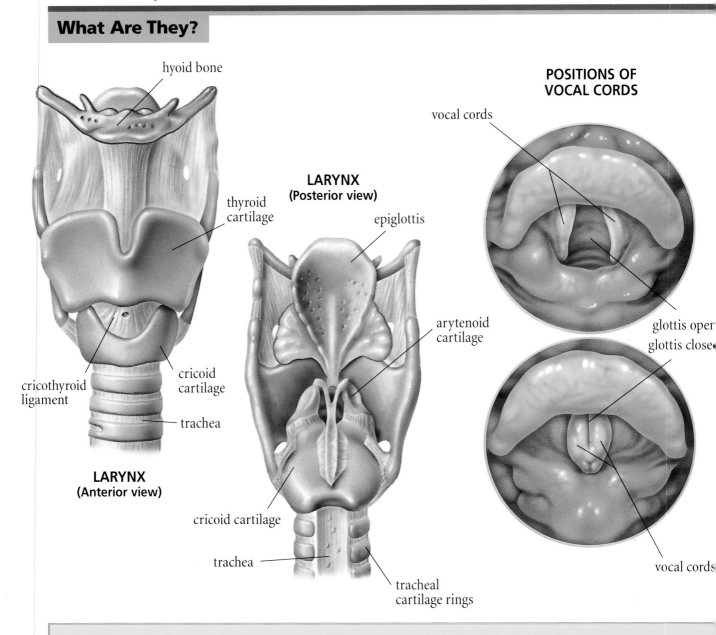

LARYNX (Posterior view)

POSITIONS OF VOCAL CORDS

hyoid bone

thyroid cartilage

cricothyroid ligament

cricoid cartilage

trachea

LARYNX (Anterior view)

epiglottis

arytenoid cartilage

cricoid cartilage

trachea

tracheal cartilage rings

vocal cords

glottis open

glottis closed

vocal cords

Larynx. The larynx forms a boxlike tunnel of curved cartilage plates. It is located between the trachea and the base of the tongue. The larynx is made up of nine cartilages and many small muscles. It measures about 1.2-1.6 inches (3-4 cm) long. The epiglottis is in the upper part of the larynx. It prevents food from entering the airway. Normally, the epiglottis is up, so that the larynx is wide open to enable comfortable breathing. The epiglottis shuts down only when food is swallowed.

Vocal cords. The vocal cords are two bands of elastic tissue, lined with a mucous membrane, that cross the interior of the larynx. The space between the vocal cords is called the glottis. When at rest, as in quiet breathing, the glottis takes on a triangular shape. Air passes through the glottis without making sound.

Speech. For humans to speak, many muscles of the larynx must work together with the cartilage plates to move the vocal cords closer together, more or less, depending on the desired sound. Then, exhaled air is forced through the glottis, vibrating the cords and producing sounds. When humans speak, the flow of air through the larynx slows down.

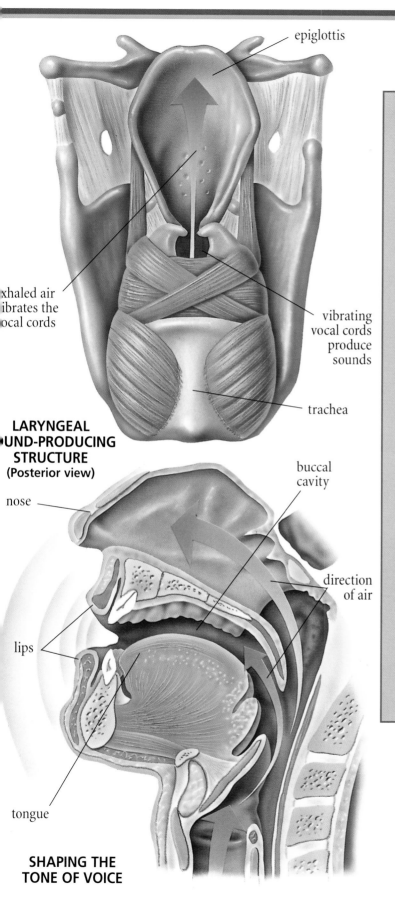

epiglottis

exhaled air
vibrates the
vocal cords

vibrating
vocal cords
produce
sounds

trachea

**LARYNGEAL
SOUND-PRODUCING
STRUCTURE**
(Posterior view)

buccal
cavity

nose

direction
of air

lips

tongue

**SHAPING THE
TONE OF VOICE**

Shaping the tone of voice. To produce speech, the mouth, lips, tongue, and teeth shape the sounds made by the vocal cords.

Exhaled air produces sounds by vibrating the vocal cords in the larynx. Air passes through a space known as the glottis that lies between the vocal cords.

When the glottis is tightened and reduced, the flow of air changes between the vocal cords. The cords vibrate, producing the sound of speech.

This sound resonates in the nose and mouth cavities. It is shaped into words by the tongue, lips, and teeth.

Differences in pitch. Men's voices are deeper than women's because men have a larger larynx, with vocal cords that can measure 3/4-1 inch (20-25 millimeters) long. The vocal cords of women and children are about 3/16 inch (5 mm) shorter, and they are farther apart.

Individual voices. The tone, intensity, timber, and other individual and unique characteristics of a person's voice depend on the shapes of the nose, the tongue, the teeth, the palate, the cheeks, the larynx, and the pharynx.

Each person's voice is different from the next. The differences allow people to recognize each other by their voices, even over the telephone.

The Trachea and Bronchi

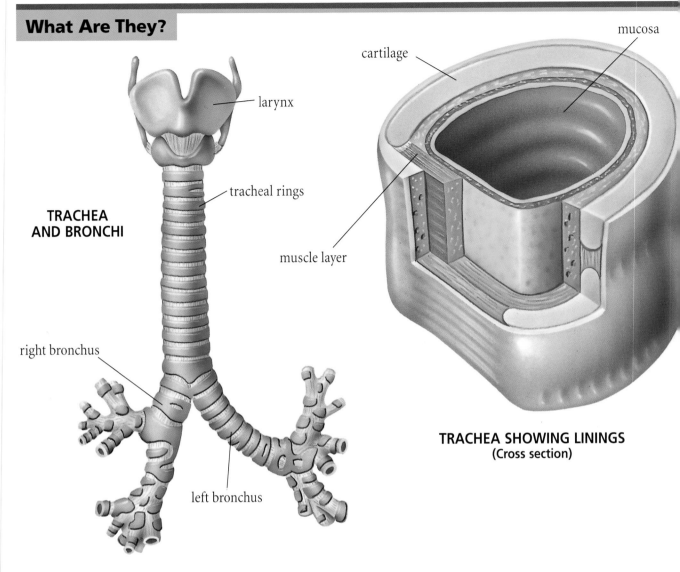

larynx

tracheal rings

TRACHEA AND BRONCHI

right bronchus

left bronchus

cartilage

mucosa

muscle layer

TRACHEA SHOWING LININGS
(Cross section)

Breathing tubes. The trachea is a tube 4-6 inches (10-15 cm) long. It is located between the larynx and the lungs. It is stiffened by C-shaped cartilage rings lined with mucous membrane similar to the lining of the nasal fossae. The upper trachea has no cartilage. Instead, its smooth muscle fibers can change the diameter of the trachea.

The partial cartilage rings are elastic and flexible, and they are constantly moving. During inhalation, they expand and elongate. During exhalation, they contract and shorten.

The trachea's inner wall has numerous cells that produce mucus, and other cells with tiny, hairlike cilia that sweep away any small particles that enter during inhalation. The undulating movements of the tracheal cartilages help expel foreign bodies, such as dust and pollen, from the airway.

At its lower end, the trachea divides into the right and left primary bronchi, each leading to one of the two lungs. The bronchi possess cartilage rings and a mucous lining.

Inside the lung, the bronchi continue to divide into ever smaller branches and finally into very narrow bronchioles that reach into every part of the lung.

This entire branching bronchi structure is called the bronchial tree. It was named this because it looks like an upside-down tree.

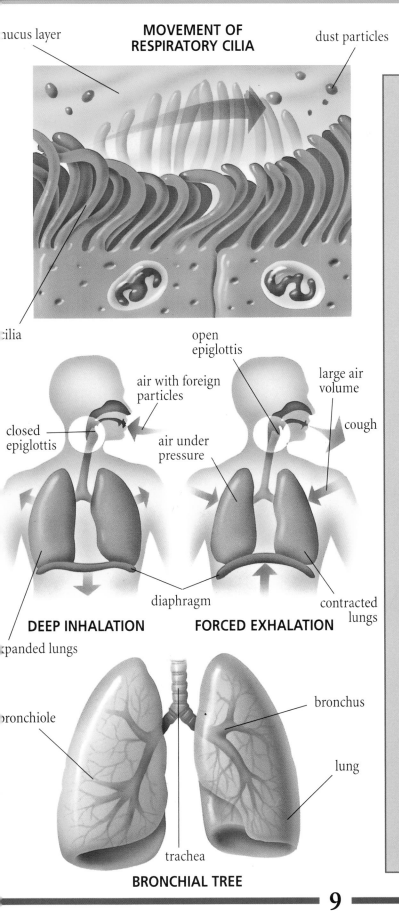

MOVEMENT OF RESPIRATORY CILIA

mucus layer

dust particles

cilia

closed epiglottis

air with foreign particles

open epiglottis

air under pressure

large air volume

cough

diaphragm

contracted lungs

DEEP INHALATION

FORCED EXHALATION

expanded lungs

bronchiole

bronchus

lung

trachea

BRONCHIAL TREE

Preparing air for the lungs. Before entering the lungs, air that is breathed in is heated, filtered, and moistened. On its way to the lungs, air continually takes on moisture from the mucous membrane that covers the upper airway. This prevents air from drying the lower airway. The air also absorbs heat from the mucosa, where the blood supply is maintained at the body temperature of 98.6° Fahrenheit (37° Centigrade).

Sweeping cilia. The membrane lining the airway produces mucus to trap tiny particles, such as dust. Ciliated cells of the mucous membrane constantly sweep the mucus, together with any particles, toward the pharynx. The items are then expelled from the body by sneezing or coughing.

The cough reflex. Coughing consists of a series of reflex actions that keep the airway free from particles, such as microorganisms, pollen, or dust. Outside particles inhaled with air set the coughing reflex in motion.

First, a deep breath fills the lungs and closes the epiglottis to build up air pressure. Then the glottis opens suddenly to release air at a speed of over 60 miles (100 kilometers) per hour, forcing the invading particles out through the mouth.

Sneezing works similarly. It is caused by irritation that stimulates the nasal mucosa. During a sneeze, strong and forcible exhalation takes place.

The bronchial tree. The trachea divides into two bronchi, each leading into a lung. The bronchi keep dividing until they form thousands of bronchioles, each thinner than a hair.

The Lungs

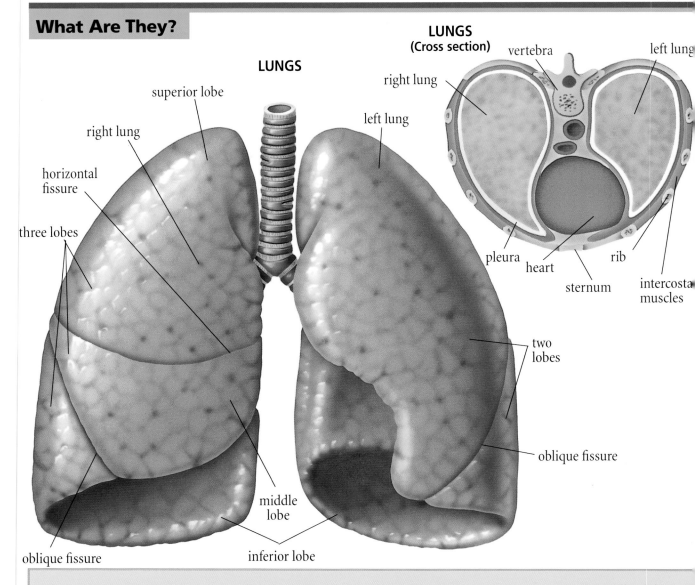

LUNGS

superior lobe

right lung

horizontal fissure

three lobes

oblique fissure

middle lobe

inferior lobe

left lung

two lobes

oblique fissure

LUNGS
(Cross section)

vertebra

left lung

right lung

left lung

pleura

heart

rib

sternum

intercostal muscles

Supplying the body with air. The lungs are two elastic and spongy masses that can expand and contract, following the movements of the thoracic muscles. The lungs, just like the heart, are well protected inside the thoracic cage, which is formed by the vertebral column, the ribs, and the sternum.

The left lung is a little longer, but smaller, than the right one. Deep fissures in the pulmonary tissue divide the lungs into lobes. The right lung is divided into three lobes; the left is divided into two. The back of the left lung has a depression in which the heart lies.

The bronchioles become smaller as they continue to branch until they end in tiny sacs called pulmonary alveoli. At these sacs, the red blood cells deliver carbon dioxide and take on oxygen from the freshly inhaled air.

The lungs of an adult have a capacity of about 5 quarts (5 liters) of air, but not all of this amount is inhaled or exhaled. When at rest, people draw in and let out about a half quart (0.5 liter) of air. During exercise, people breathe in about 2 quarts (2 liters) of air at a time. The air from the lungs is not entirely replaced with freshly inhaled air.

If the lungs fill with fluid, they can no longer draw in air. Pneumonia (caused by bacterial infection) and congestive heart failure (due to weak heartbeat) can cause fluid accumulation, which is called edema.

BREATHING ACTION OF DIAPHRAGM

xhaling
(iaphragm rises to
ress the lungs)

haling
(iaphragm lowers)

diaphragm

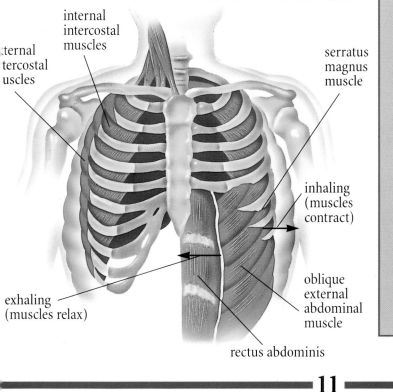

BREATHING ACTION OF INTERCOSTAL MUSCLES

internal
intercostal
muscles

:ternal
tercostal
uscles

serratus
magnus
muscle

inhaling
(muscles
contract)

oblique
external
abdominal
muscle

exhaling
(muscles relax)

rectus abdominis

Lung protection. Each lung is covered with an elastic membrane, called a pleura, which protects the lung from friction against the ribs and the other bones of the thoracic cage during respiratory movements. Each pleura is formed from a double membrane shaped like a sac with two walls. The inner layer covers the lungs, and the outer layer lines the inside of the thoracic cage and the diaphragm. No air is between the pleurae. Instead, there is a fluid that enables the two pleurae to slide against one another without any friction.

Movements of the diaphragm. The diaphragm is located between the bottom of the thoracic cage and the abdominal cavity. It is a dome-shaped muscle used in breathing. During inhalation, the diaphragm flattens and moves down. This increases the thoracic volume, the free space of the lungs in the thorax. The lungs dilate to fill with air. The diaphragm rises and pushes against the ribs and lungs, forcing the air out.

Intercostal muscles. Two other groups of muscles act during breathing. While inhaling, the intercostal muscles contract and pull the ribs upward; the diaphragm contracts at the same time. In exhaling, the intercostal muscles and diaphragm relax in order to release the air.

This is nearly automatic, for the muscles relax at the end of drawing in a breath, and the lungs and thorax move to expel the air.

To force air out, as when blowing, the internal intercostal muscles pull the ribs down while the abdominal muscles push the diaphragm up.

The Bronchioles and Alveoli

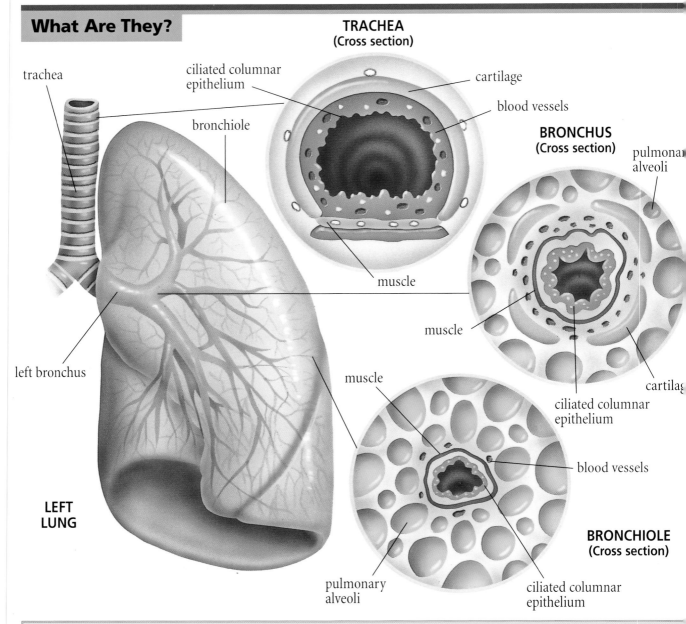

TRACHEA
(Cross section)

trachea

ciliated columnar
epithelium

cartilage

blood vessels

bronchiole

BRONCHUS
(Cross section)

pulmonar
alveoli

muscle

muscle

left bronchus

muscle

ciliated columnar
epithelium

cartilag

blood vessels

LEFT
LUNG

pulmonary
alveoli

ciliated columnar
epithelium

BRONCHIOLE
(Cross section)

Looking deeper inside. Inside the lobes in each lung, the bronchi branch further. The bronchus of the left lung branches into lobular bronchi. The bronchus of the right lung branches further into three lobular bronchi, each leading to one of the three lobes.

Inside the lungs, the bronchi keep branching and narrowing. Eventually, they become ducts of less than 0.04 inch (1 mm) in diameter. These are called bronchioles.

The bronchioles end in alveoli, the tiny sacs that form pulmonary tissue. The bronchioles are still covered with ciliated cells, but these gradually disappear as they get closer to the alveoli, which are covered with flat, or squamous, cells. Alveoli are tiny sacs where a gas exchange takes place with red blood cells.

The sacs are grouped in clusters, like bunches of grapes. Every alveolus is surrounded by a network of capillaries so tiny that blood cells must go through them in single file.

Each lung contains 300 million alveoli. Among these are tiny capillaries with walls made of epithelial cells. The separation between blood and air is only 0.00002 inch (0.0005 mm).

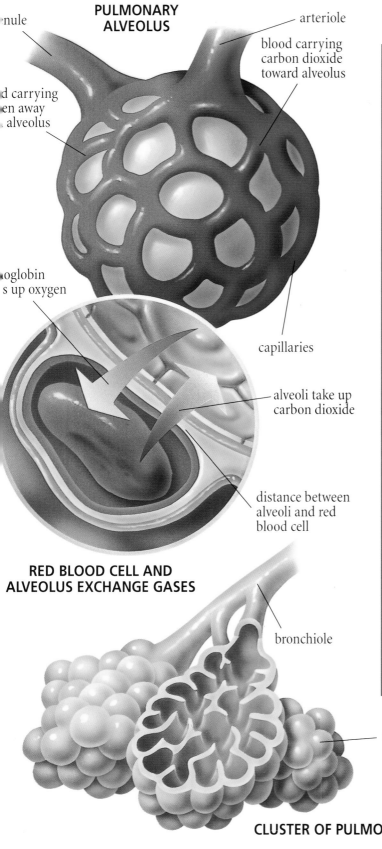

PULMONARY ALVEOLUS

nule

arteriole

blood carrying carbon dioxide toward alveolus

d carrying en away alveolus

oglobin s up oxygen

capillaries

alveoli take up carbon dioxide

distance between alveoli and red blood cell

RED BLOOD CELL AND ALVEOLUS EXCHANGE GASES

bronchiole

alveolus

CLUSTER OF PULMONARY ALVEOLI

Pulmonary alveolus. The body's cells use oxygen to burn food. The food is transformed into energy that the body needs. This transformation produces carbon dioxide, a waste gas that can be toxic. Hemoglobin in the red blood cells carries carbon dioxide from cells to alveoli for disposal outside the body.

The amount, or concentration, of oxygen in inhaled air is greater than in the capillaries. The concentration of carbon dioxide in capillaries is greater than in freshly inhaled air. Each gas moves through the alveolar wall in order to balance its own pressure on both sides. Oxygen passes into the red blood cells, and carbon dioxide passes into the alveoli in a continual exchange of gases.

Rapid exchange of gases. Inhaled air reaches the alveoli, where red blood cells take up oxygen. The red blood cells carry the oxygen to all the cells throughout the body. Hemoglobin in the red blood cells contains iron. This iron binds to the molecules of oxygen. Needed oxygen is released at every cell of the body. Carbon dioxide from each cell's respiration is carried by the blood to the capillaries surrounding the alveoli. These ducts are very narrow. At this point, the alveolus is less than 0.00002 inch (0.0005 mm) away. Because of this extremely tiny distance, the gases are able to exchange very rapidly.

The Circulation of Blood

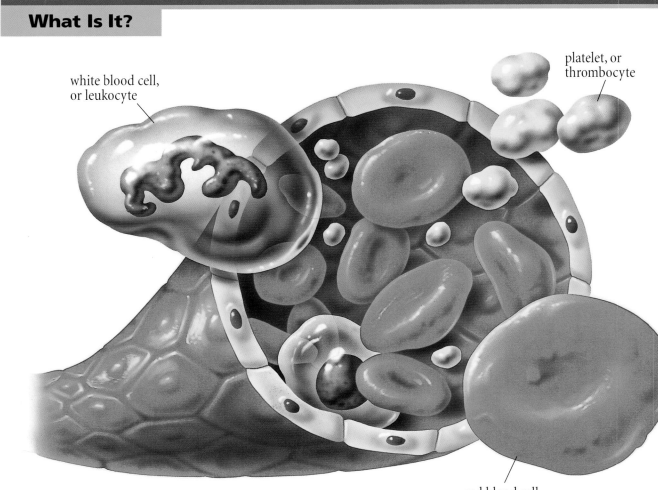

white blood cell, or leukocyte

platelet, or thrombocyte

red blood cell, or erythrocyte

BLOOD VESSEL AND CORPUSCLES

Traveling throughout the body. The circulatory system is a network that consists of the heart and the blood vessels. The two kinds of blood vessels are arteries and veins. Every day about 4-6 quarts (4-6 liters) of blood pass through the heart more than a thousand times.

Blood is a red and viscous fluid that travels through the network of arteries, veins, and capillaries in the body. It carries needed oxygen and nutrients to all the body's cells.

Blood also collects the waste products of the cells to be expelled by the body through the lungs as carbon dioxide and through the kidneys as urine. Adults have around 5 quarts (5 liters) of blood, which is

being constantly pumped through the heart. Observed under a microscope, blood contains a straw-colored fluid, called blood plasma, in which the different kinds of cells, or corpuscles, are suspended. Plasma is 90 percent water. About half of blood is plasma.

Blood absorbs heat well, and it is also a good means of transportation. Besides blood cells, plasma carries other substances, such as proteins, sugars, metals, minerals, hormones, and antibodies.

The blood cells are: erythrocytes, or red blood cells; leukocytes, or white blood cells; and thrombocytes, or platelets. Each type of cell performs its own individual function in the body.

CLOTTING

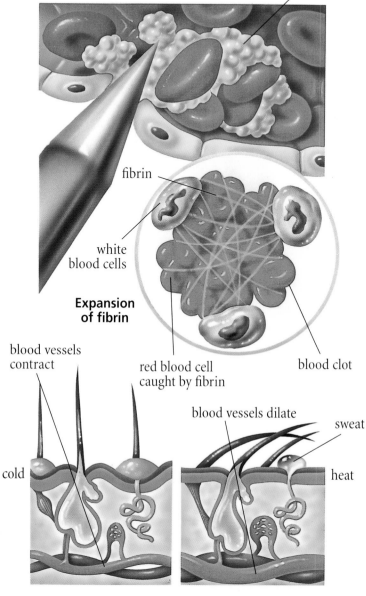

platelets close wound

fibrin

white
blood cells

**Expansion
of fibrin**

blood vessels
contract

red blood cell
caught by fibrin

blood clot

cold

blood vessels dilate

sweat

heat

BLOOD VESSEL REACTS TO TEMPERATURE

VASOCONSTRICTION
(Contraction of injured blood vessel)

Clotting. Platelets, or thrombocytes, start the clotting process. Each cubic 0.00006 inch (1 cubic mm) of blood contains approximately 150,000-300,000 platelets. These are very tiny, flat cell particles that do not have a nucleus. They are formed in bone marrow from very large cells called megakaryocytes. Megakaryocyte's cytoplasm (non-nucleated substance) fragments into numerous small particles called platelets.

When capillaries rupture, the newly rough surface causes platelets to become sticky and adhere to the edges of the break and to each other. The platelets form a barrier, or plug, that closes the break. Capillary ruptures happen often. The platelet plugs readily seal these breaks, but they are too small to plug breaks in larger vessels, where greater blood flow can wash them away.

Cold and heat. During cold weather, blood vessels in the skin contract to retain heat. During hot weather, blood vessels dilate to increase body cooling.

Vasoconstriction. When a large vessel is severed, the muscles in its wall contract because of a substance released by nearby platelets. This vasoconstriction reduces the vessel's diameter so that the smaller opening can then be blocked by a blood clot. A damaged surface starts the clotting process within 15-20 seconds after injury. Fibrin, a threadlike protein, forms a mesh, or net, at the break. This traps red blood cells, forming a dam across the break. The clot dissolves during healing.

The Red and White Blood Cells

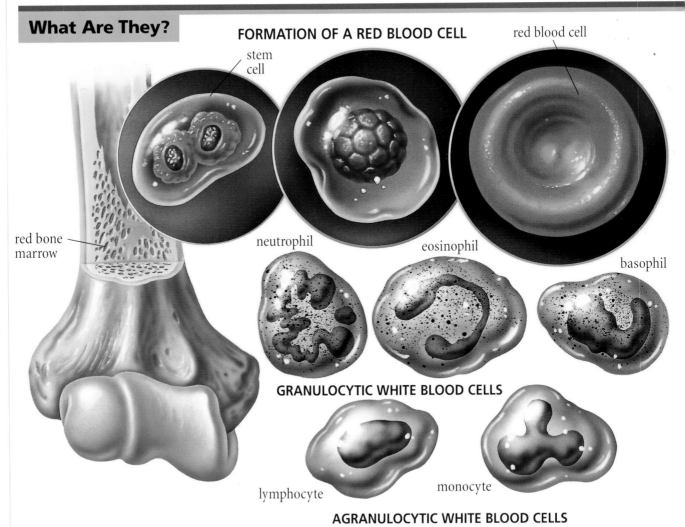

FORMATION OF A RED BLOOD CELL

stem cell

red blood cell

red bone marrow

neutrophil

eosinophil

basophil

GRANULOCYTIC WHITE BLOOD CELLS

lymphocyte

monocyte

AGRANULOCYTIC WHITE BLOOD CELLS

Red blood cells. Red blood cells are disk-shaped with a thin center and thicker rim. When a red cell matures, its nucleus disappears. Red cells are the most numerous blood cells. They take up about 45 percent of blood volume. Plasma, the blood's fluid, carries the cells through the body. The red cell has hemoglobin, a protein containing iron molecules that bind to oxygen in order to carry the oxygen. Iron also colors the blood cell red.

Red blood cells form in the red bone marrow of the ribs, sternum, and the ends of long bones. The stem cells of the red marrow develop into all the types of blood cells, mostly erythrocytes. The body produces several million new erythrocytes per second, each living only 120 days. Every second, millions of aging erythrocytes are destroyed by the liver and spleen. Their iron is used in making new erythrocytes.

White blood cells. Leukocytes, or white blood cells, fight invasions of pathogens. They are larger than erythrocytes and have a nucleus. Each 0.00006 cubic inch (1 cubic mm) of blood contains 5,000-10,000 white blood cells, which are colorless until stained for examination.

The two kinds of leukocytes are granulocytes and agranulocytes. Granulocytes contain granules and are produced in the red bone marrow. The kinds of granulocytes are neutrophils, eosinophils, and basophils. Neutrophils, the most active infection fighters, make up 60-70 percent of white cells. Agranulocytes, without granules, are produced in lymphatic tissue in the spleen and thymus, and in red bone marrow. The two kinds of agranulocytes are lymphocytes and monocytes. Lymphocytes, 20-30 percent of white cells, migrate to lymph nodes.

PHAGOCYTOSIS

invasive agent

pseudopods that move the white blood cells

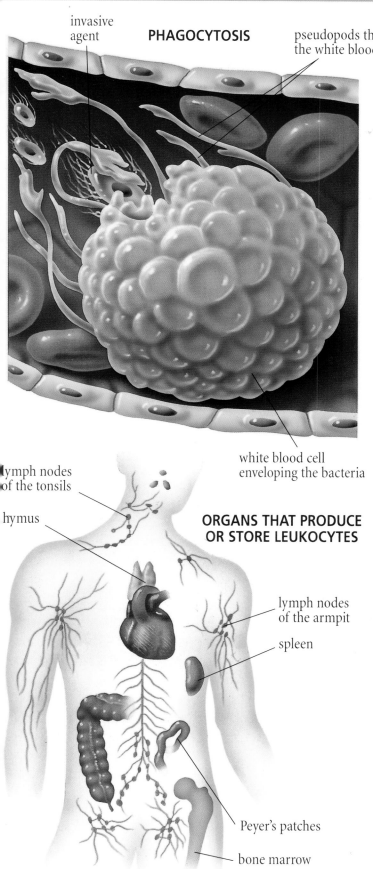

white blood cell enveloping the bacteria

ORGANS THAT PRODUCE OR STORE LEUKOCYTES

lymph nodes of the tonsils

thymus

lymph nodes of the armpit

spleen

Peyer's patches

bone marrow

Phagocytosis. Unlike red blood cells, white blood cells can move themselves, using pseudopods. White blood cells can wriggle through the walls of blood vessels to reach the body's tissues, where they search for bacterial invaders. Some white blood cells inside the blood vessels circulate with the bloodstream, but most marginate, or cling, to the inside walls.

When a bacterium or other foreign body is detected, a leukocyte approaches rapidly and engulfs the bacterium by extending armlike pseudopods and pulling the bacterium inside its cytoplasm. There, it digests the bacterium. This maneuver is called phagocytosis.

Granulocytic leukocytes live only a couple of days. Pus forms from leukocytes that die while fighting bacteria, from dead and living bacteria, and from cellular waste suspended in lymph.

Aging cells. Leukocytes remove aging red blood cells from circulation by engulfing and digesting them.

Producing leukocytes. When an infection (such as appendicitis) occurs, the body responds by increasing its number of leukocytes to battle it.

red blood cell

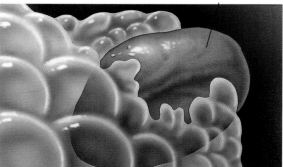

LEUKOCYTE ENGULFING A RED BLOOD CELL

The Heart

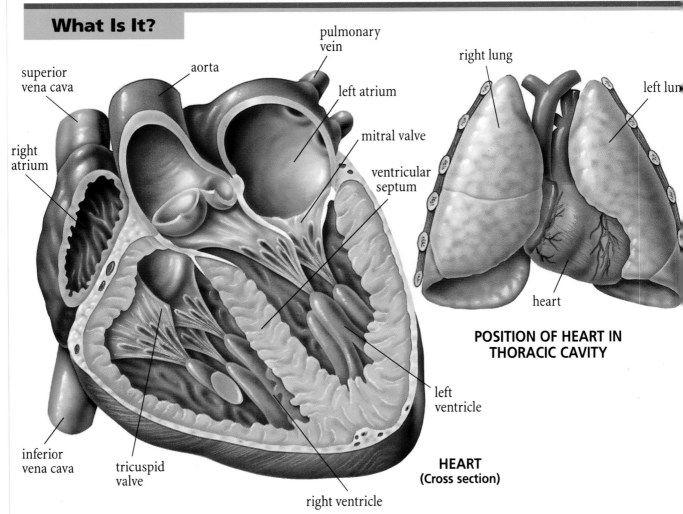

superior
vena cava

aorta

pulmonary
vein

left atrium

right lung

left lung

right
atrium

mitral valve

ventricular
septum

inferior
vena cava

tricuspid
valve

right ventricle

left
ventricle

heart

**POSITION OF HEART IN
THORACIC CAVITY**

**HEART
(Cross section)**

Pumping blood. The heart is a hollow, muscular organ that pumps blood through the body. Approximately cone-shaped, it's located between the lungs, just above the diaphragm, mostly on the left side. Three pericardial membranes, two separated by fluid, cushion the beating heart from friction.

The heart is made from cardiac muscle, called myocardium, and it weighs about 8-12 ounces (227-340 grams). Inside, the heart is divided into four chambers. A central wall, or septum, divides it vertically, and a constriction separates the upper part of each half.

The upper chambers are the right and left atria; the lower chambers are the right and left ventricles. The two thin-walled atria receive blood from veins, and the muscular ventricles pump it out into arteries. The central septum keeps blood on the two sides from mixing. Cardiac valves, composed of endocardium and connective tissue, keep blood flowing in one direction.

The right atrium receives unoxygenated blood from the body through two large veins, the superior vena cava and inferior vena cava. The blood flows through the tricuspid valve into the right ventricle. The right ventricle contracts, pumping the blood to the lungs, where it releases carbon dioxide and takes on oxygen. The oxygenated blood flows through four pulmonary veins into the left atrium and passes through the mitral valve into the left ventricle. The left ventricle pumps the blood into the aorta, the body's largest artery, for circulation throughout the body. Coronary vessels supply nutrients to the heart muscle itself. If a coronary artery is blocked, part of the myocardium dies, causing a heart attack.

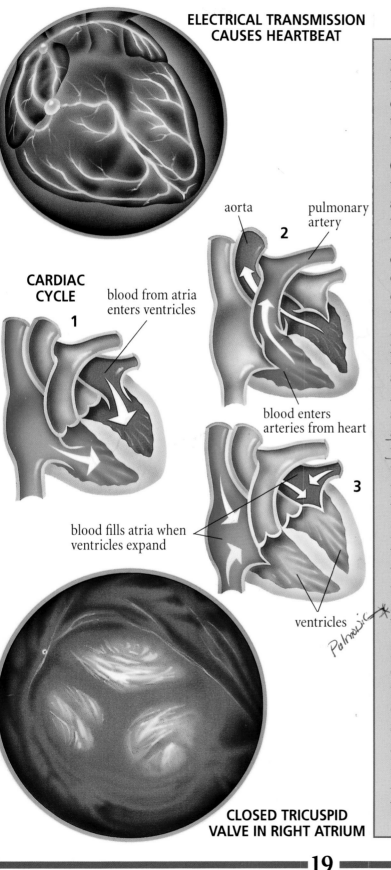

ELECTRICAL TRANSMISSION CAUSES HEARTBEAT

CARDIAC CYCLE

1 — blood from atria enters ventricles

2 — aorta / pulmonary artery / blood enters arteries from heart

blood fills atria when ventricles expand

3 — ventricles

Pulmonic

CLOSED TRICUSPID VALVE IN RIGHT ATRIUM

Heartbeat. The contractions of the heart form the heartbeat. Each contraction is caused by an electrical stimulus that travels to all the cardiac chambers from two small cell masses called nodal tissue.

Cardiac cycle. The cardiac cycle is made up of systoles and diastoles. Systoles, another name for contractions, drive the blood out of cardiac chambers into ventricles or arteries. Diastoles are dilations, the relaxed state that follows contractions. During diastole, blood enters both atria simultaneously from the vena cavae and the pulmonary veins.

Phase 1. The cardiac cycle, or heartbeat, has three phases. The first phase is the atria systole and ventricular diastole (1). After most of the blood from the filled atria flows into the dilated ventricles, the atria contract simultaneously to pump out the remaining amount. Then both the tricuspid and mitral valves close, preventing blood from flowing back into the atria.

Phase 2. The second phase includes the ventricular systole (2). Both blood-filled ventricles contract, driving the blood into the arteries, either pulmonary or the aorta. Semilunar valves in the arteries keep the blood from flowing back into the ventricles.

Phase 3. In the third phase, general diastole takes place (3). After emptying, the heart relaxes. Atria and ventricles expand, and blood flows into the atria.

The pulmonary artery from the right ventricle takes the blood to the lungs for oxygenation. The aorta from the left ventricle and its many branches carry blood throughout the body.

The Arteries

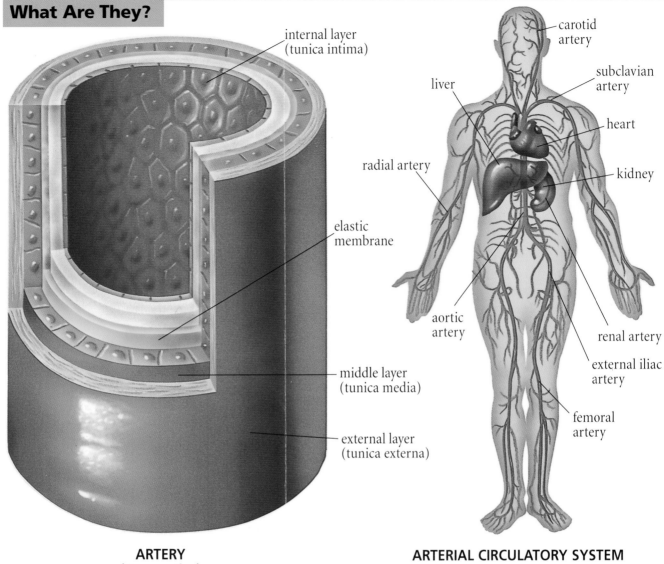

ARTERY
(Cross section)

ARTERIAL CIRCULATORY SYSTEM

Highways of the body. Arteries are the blood vessels through which blood travels from the heart to different tissues and organs in the body.

The heart forces blood through the arteries under pressure so that it can reach every part of the body. Blood pressure is greatest in the aorta, and it lessens the farther away the blood travels from the heart.

Three tissue layers, or tunicae, make up the arteries. The innermost tunica is the tunica intima, made from the same tissue that lines the heart's chambers. This layer is extremely smooth, in both heart and arteries, to prevent clots from forming. The tunica media, or middle layer, is a thick layer of smooth

muscle and elastic connective tissue that maintains normal blood pressure. The layer of smooth muscle allows arteries to dilate or constrict according to the body's need for more or less blood.

The tunica externa, or outer layer, is made from fibrous connective tissue. This layer is thick and very strong to prevent the rupture of arteries carrying blood under high pressure.

Two arteries come from the heart: the aorta, which keeps branching during the long systemic, or bodily, circulation; and the pulmonary artery, which carries blood to the lungs to be oxygenated during the shorter pulmonary circulation.

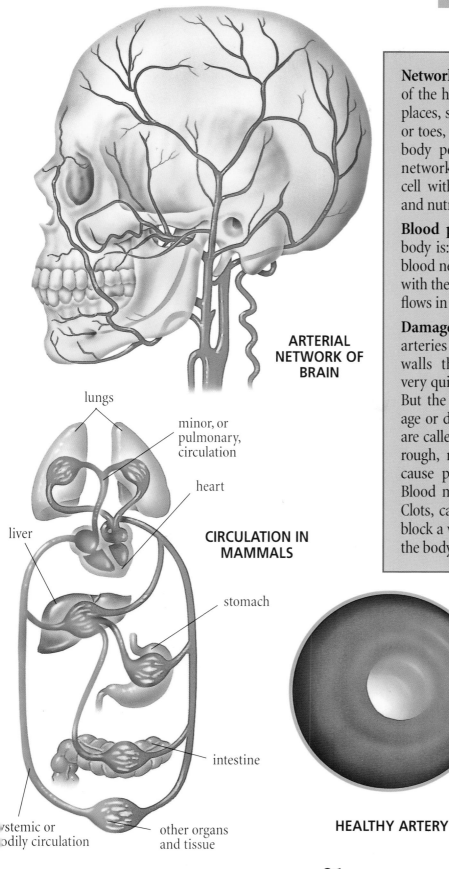

ARTERIAL NETWORK OF BRAIN

lungs

minor, or pulmonary, circulation

heart

liver

CIRCULATION IN MAMMALS

stomach

intestine

 systemic or bodily circulation

other organs and tissue

Networks. When arterial blood comes out of the heart, it can go to several different places, such as the brain, liver, intestines, or toes, for example. Some regions of the body possess a complete and complex network of arteries that supply each cell with the needed amount of oxygen and nutrients.

Blood path. Circulation of the human body is: *complete* — venous and arterial blood never mix; *closed* — has no contact with the outer world; and *double* — blood flows in two circuits.

Damaged arteries. Young and healthy arteries are elastic tubes with smooth walls through which blood circulates very quickly and with hardly any friction. But the interior of arteries changes with age or disease. Old and calcified arteries are called sclerotic. A sclerotic artery has rough, rigid, and fragile walls that can cause problems with blood circulation. Blood moves slowly in sclerotic arteries. Clots, called thrombi, can form that will block a vessel and cause severe damage to the body.

HEALTHY ARTERY　　　**DISEASED ARTERY**

The Veins

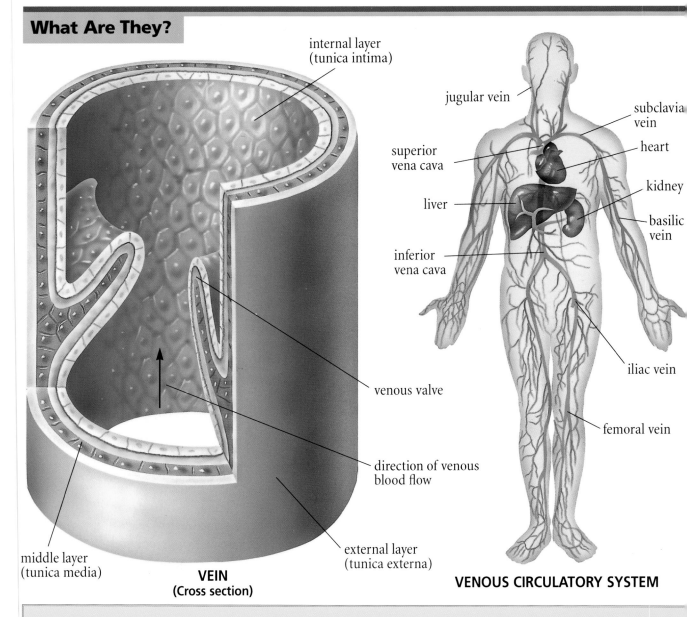

internal layer
(tunica intima)

middle layer
(tunica media)

VEIN
(Cross section)

external layer
(tunica externa)

venous valve

direction of venous
blood flow

jugular vein

subclavia
vein

superior
vena cava

heart

liver

kidney

basilic
vein

inferior
vena cava

iliac vein

femoral vein

VENOUS CIRCULATORY SYSTEM

The long way back. The body possesses a complete venous system that brings blood back to the heart from all parts where the arterial vessels have taken it. The structure of veins and arteries is alike, for they both have three overlapping layers of tissue. However, the tunica media and the tunica externa of veins are much thinner because they do not regulate blood pressure. Blood in veins does not have as much pressure as in arteries because veins are so far away from the beating heart.

The endothelium that lines the veins is folded to form valves that prevent blood from backing up, especially in the veins of the legs. Veins are softer, more fragile, and less elastic than arteries. Veins are distributed in the body parallel to arteries. Nearly all veins carry venous blood, which is poor in oxygen and loaded with carbon dioxide, the residue from cellular respiration. When the concentration of carbon dioxide increases, the hemoglobin of red blood cells turns from red to purplish-blue, the color typical of venous blood.

The only veins that send arterial blood to the heart are pulmonary veins. These veins come from the lungs and transport oxygenated blood directly to the heart. From there, it is pumped through the body, bringing needed oxygen to the cells.

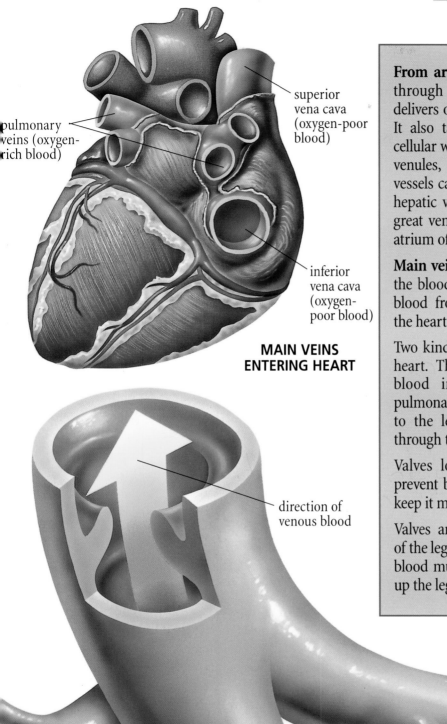

pulmonary veins (oxygen-rich blood)

superior vena cava (oxygen-poor blood)

inferior vena cava (oxygen-poor blood)

MAIN VEINS ENTERING HEART

direction of venous blood

venule

VEIN
(Cross section)

From arteries to veins. After traveling through the arterial network, blood delivers oxygen and nutrients to the cells. It also takes away carbon dioxide and cellular wastes. The blood then enters the venules, which join to form ever larger vessels called veins, such as the renal and hepatic veins. Finally, blood reaches the great vena cavae, which lead to the right atrium of the heart.

Main veins to heart. The function of all the blood vessels called veins is to carry blood from other parts of the body to the heart.

Two kinds of veins enter the atria in the heart. The vena cavae bring oxygen-poor blood into the right atrium. The pulmonary veins bring oxygen-rich blood to the left atrium after it has passed through the lungs.

Valves located inside the larger veins prevent blood from flowing backward, to keep it moving in the right direction.

Valves are most numerous in the veins of the legs. This is very important because blood must fight against gravity to move up the legs toward the heart.

The Capillary Circulation

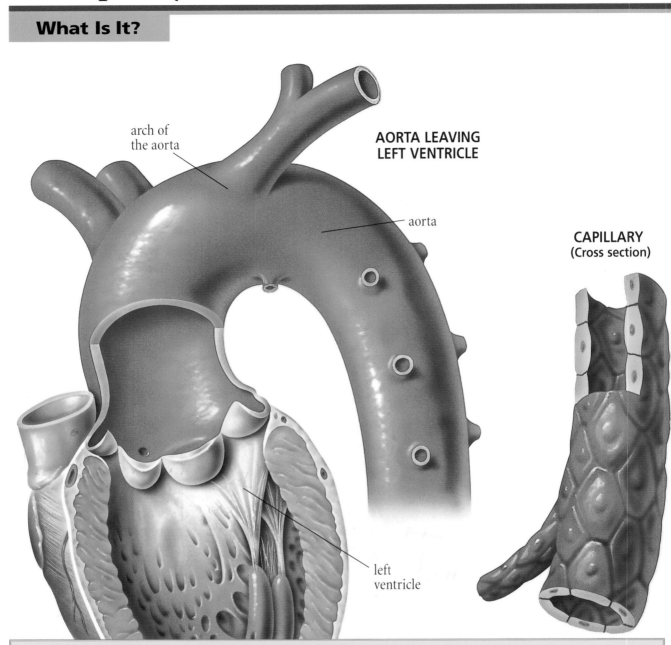

arch of
the aorta

**AORTA LEAVING
LEFT VENTRICLE**

aorta

**CAPILLARY
(Cross section)**

left
ventricle

The smallest blood vessels. The capillary network lies between the arterial and venous circulatory systems. Blood starts and ends its long journey in the heart, flowing through organs and cells for a distance of thousands of miles (kilometers). Every 60 seconds, about 1,440 times a day, blood makes a complete circuit around the body. Oxygenated blood starts its journey from the left ventricle, which pumps it into the aorta.

The aorta rises from the left ventricle, curves back over the heart, travels down the thorax, and goes through the diaphragm into the abdomen. On the way, smaller arteries continually branch off to reach into every organ and part of the body.

Within each organ, arteries continue to branch, becoming smaller until they form the capillary network. This network supplies all cells with nutrients. Besides oxygen, blood carries hormones produced in glands; ions, such as sodium, chloride, and potassium; nutrients, such as vitamins, fats, sugars, proteins, and minerals; and other substances vital for all cells of the body.

SUBSTANCE EXCHANGE ACROSS CAPILLARY WALLS

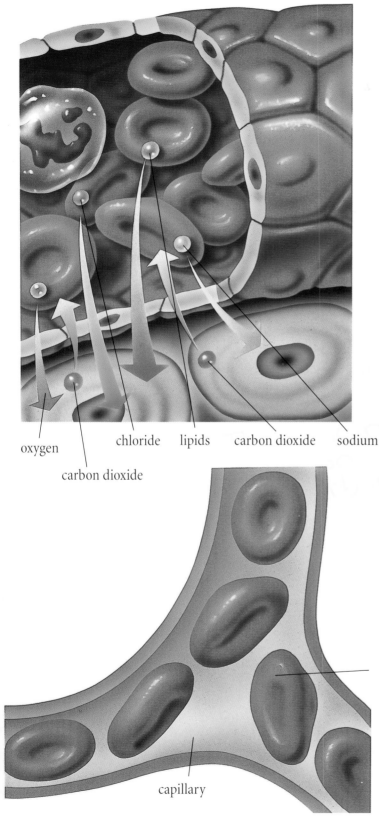

oxygen

carbon dioxide

chloride lipids carbon dioxide sodium

Capillary networks. Most tissues have a network of capillaries so complete and dense that no cell is farther than 0.000016 inch (0.0004 mm) from the nearest source of blood. After the exchange of nutrients and wastes with the tissue cells, capillaries become venules, and the blood starts its return to the heart.

Exchanges. Blood pressure in the capillaries forces plasma, and the nutrients it carries, out into the tissue fluid. There, capillaries and cells exchange substances, such as minerals, ions, and gases. Red blood cells deliver nutrients and oxygen to all tissue cells. The adjoining venule section of the capillary network absorbs most tissue fluid. There, red blood cells take up cellular waste products and some carbon dioxide. Most carbon dioxide dissolves in plasma for transfer to the lungs. The exchange of gases, carbon dioxide for oxygen, takes place in the cells, in a process known as cellular respiration.

Single file. Capillary walls are formed by only a single cell layer. Capillaries are so thin that red blood cells have to go through one by one. This makes it easier for red blood cells to exchange substances and gases with the cells of the tissues through which they pass.

red blood cells
twist in order to
pass one by one

capillary

RED BLOOD CELLS FILING THROUGH A CAPILLARY

The Pulmonary Circulation

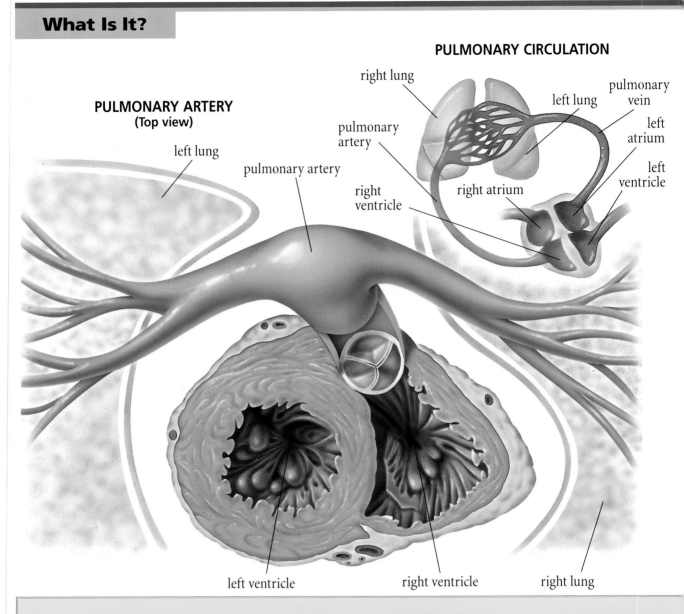

PULMONARY CIRCULATION

right lung

pulmonary vein

left lung

left atrium

pulmonary artery

left ventricle

right ventricle

right atrium

PULMONARY ARTERY
(Top view)

left lung

pulmonary artery

left ventricle

right ventricle

right lung

Taking up oxygen. Pulmonary circulation is the journey blood makes from the heart's right ventricle to the lungs, and back to the heart. The thinner walls of the right ventricle pump with only one-sixth of the force that the left ventricle uses. This low blood pressure in the pulmonary arteries and capillaries keeps plasma from leaking into the alveoli and accumulating there, preventing the intake of oxygen.

Blood entering the pulmonary artery from the right ventricle is low in oxygen and high in carbon dioxide. The pulmonary artery divides into two branches, each leading to one of the lungs. There, each branch continues dividing into finer vessels to form a network of capillaries. Blood circulates slowly through the capillaries to allow the exchange of gases in the pulmonary alveoli. In a day of normal breathing, an alveolus fills with air and empties over 15,000 times.

The lungs contain around 300 million alveoli, each surrounded by a capillary network. Oxygen from the air breathed in passes through the alveolar walls and into the capillaries. From there, it flows into the pulmonary veins. When the oxygenated blood reaches the left atrium, it passes into the left ventricle. From there, it is pumped to all the cells in the body to supply them with oxygen.

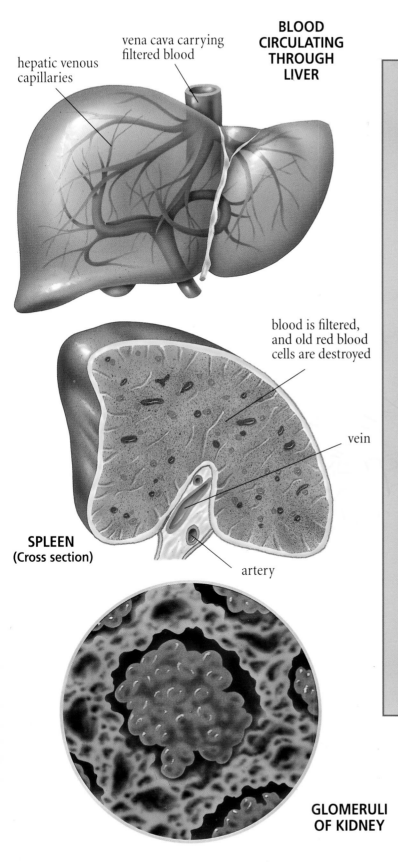

BLOOD CIRCULATING THROUGH LIVER

hepatic venous capillaries

vena cava carrying filtered blood

blood is filtered, and old red blood cells are destroyed

vein

SPLEEN (Cross section)

artery

GLOMERULI OF KIDNEY

Liver. The liver is the largest organ in the human body, weighing about 2.4-3.75 pounds (1.1-1.7 kilograms). It is made up of about 50,000 to 100,000 hepatic lobules, which are tiny cylinders of hepatic tissue around a central vein. Blood from the digestive organs and spleen goes through the portal vein and the liver before returning to the heart.

The large portal vein branches into smaller venules and capillaries to the hepatic lobules. The lobule cells filter the blood. The filtered blood then returns to the heart through veins.

Spleen. The spleen is an organ weighing around 7 ounces (200 grams). It is located on the left side of the body just under the diaphragm. It receives blood from the splenic artery and sends it to the liver. Splenic cells engulf old erythrocytes and pathogens. The spleen helps form bile and also produces antibodies.

Kidney. The renal artery and vein enter the kidney in the center of its concave side. About one million glomeruli in each kidney filter the blood that passes through. The nephron — a tiny, complex tubular structure surrounded with a network of capillaries — forms urine from the glomerular filtrate fluid and waste products. Urine collects in the bladder and leaves the body through the urethra.

The Lymphatic System

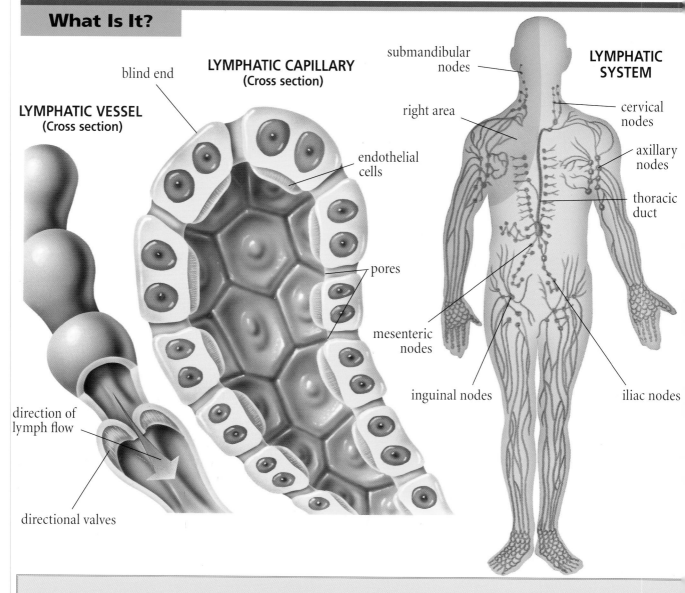

LYMPHATIC VESSEL
(Cross section)

blind end

LYMPHATIC CAPILLARY
(Cross section)

endothelial cells

pores

direction of lymph flow

directional valves

submandibular nodes

LYMPHATIC SYSTEM

right area

cervical nodes

axillary nodes

thoracic duct

mesenteric nodes

inguinal nodes

iliac nodes

Lymph. Most tissue fluid, which comes from blood plasma, leaves by a process of uptake in blood capillaries. The remaining tissue fluid enters the system of lymphatic vessels, which are extremely thin-walled. This fluid, now called lymph, travels through lymphatic vessels and returns to the circulating blood to maintain normal blood pressure. Lymphatic vessels collect proteins and the fat-soluble products of digestion, such as vitamin A and the fatty acids. Fats in suspension give lymph a milky appearance. Lymph also contains white blood cells, or lymphocytes.

Lymphatic vessels (capillaries) are always close to blood capillaries. The lymphatic capillaries merge to form ever larger vessels, just as the venous system does. Lymph eventually flows into large veins near the heart, entering the blood circulation, where it becomes plasma again.

The lymphatic system does not have a pump. Lymph keeps moving through its vessels in the same way that blood moves through the veins. The smooth muscle layer in the larger lymph vessels constricts to push the lymph onward, and one-way valves keep this fluid moving in a single direction. Muscles in the arms and legs pump the lymph by squeezing the lymph vessels located in the limbs. The chest cavity moves lymph when it expands and contracts during breathing.

FLOW FROM BLOOD CAPILLARIES INTO LYMPHATIC CAPILLARIES

lymphocytes

blood
capillary

interstitial
fluid

lymphatic
capillary

afferent
lymphatic vessel

efferent
lymphatic vessel

**LYMPH
NODE**

Fluid flow. The ends of lymphatic capillaries are blind, or closed. Fluid passes easily into these very thin capillaries. Lymph carries some proteins, large molecules of fat digestion, and fat-soluble vitamins to nourish some tissues without a blood supply, such as cartilage.

Lymph nodes. The lymphatic system protects the body from infection. Lymph tissue masses to form nodes about 0.4-0.8 inch (10-20 mm) long and smaller nodules. Nodes are grouped along the lymphatic vessels. Lymph enters a node through several vessels, and exits through one or two vessels.

Inside the node, lymph flows through a meshlike tissue that traps pathogens. Macrophages inside the nodes engulf and destroy the pathogens, while lymphocytes make antibodies against them. Eventually, these antibodies, lymphocytes, and monocytes enter the bloodstream.

Swollen "glands" are the nodes in the groin, armpit, and neck that become overworked in battling infection. Tonsils and adenoids are formed from lymph nodes. Lymph nodules around body openings help prevent entry of pathogens.

Glossary

alveoli — the tiny air sacs of the lungs where gas exchange takes place.

aorta — the largest artery in the body that travels from the heart down through the abdomen.

arteries — vessels that carry blood, usually oxygenated, away from the heart. The smallest arteries are arterioles.

atrium — one of two upper chambers of the heart that receive blood and send it to a ventricle.

bacteria — single-celled microorganisms of various species. Some are useful, but many can cause disease.

bronchi — tubes that carry air into and out of the lungs. Bronchi branch and decrease in size to become bronchioles.

bronchial tree — the entire structure of airways, formed by branching bronchial tubes and alveoli, that resembles an upside-down tree.

buccal — related to the mouth.

capillaries — the thin blood vessels that connect the arterial and venous systems. Exchanges of material often occur in capillary networks.

carbon dioxide — a toxic waste gas produced by cells using oxygen to metabolize nutrients.

cartilage — a strong, white tissue more flexible than bone, found in joints and such structures as the trachea, outer ears, and nostrils. In a developing baby, most of the skeleton is cartilage that is gradually replaced by bone.

cilia — thin, movable filaments projecting from a cell membrane; sometimes called cell hairs.

cytoplasm — the main substance of a cell that surrounds the nucleus and carries on the vital cellular processes.

diastole dilation — relaxation period of the heart. During this time, the heart expands and fills with blood flowing in through the great pulmonary veins and vena cavae.

epiglottis — a movable cartilage flap that covers the larynx during swallowing.

epithelium — the layer of cells that covers the inner and outer surface of an organ of the body. It makes up the skin and mucous membranes.

erythrocytes — red blood cells.

fibrin — insoluble protein that forms the essential portion of a blood clot.

glomerulus — a capillary network in the nephron, the working unit of the kidney. Glomeruli remove wastes and toxins from the blood.

hemoglobin — a protein inside the red blood cell, formed by four heme groups (molecules containing iron) that hold the oxygen to be transported.

ions — atoms, or groups of atoms and molecules, that have acquired an electric charge by gaining or losing an electron.

larynx — the structure at the top of the trachea that contains the vocal cords.

leukocytes — white blood cells.

ligament — a tough, cordlike structure of fibrous connective tissue that connects bone to bone.

lymph — tissue fluid carried by thin-walled lymphatic vessels to be returned to the circulating blood near the heart.

macrophage — a type of white cell that can engulf and destroy pathogens, damaged cells, and aged red blood cells.

molecule — a combination of two or more atoms that forms the smallest structure of a substance with a particular identity.

mucosa — tissues that cover the inside of the body's cavities. The buccal mucosa covers the inside of the mouth.

nasal fossae — nasal cavities.

olfactory cells — the cells of the nasal fossae that respond to odors.

palate — the structure separating the mouth from the nasal fossae.

peristalsis — one-way waves of muscle contraction that push contents onward.

phagocytosis — the process of a cell engulfing a particle or microorganism.

plasma — the clear fluid of blood in which blood cells are suspended.

platelets — small, non-nucleated fragments of a larger cell that plug breaks in blood vessels.

pleura — the membrane that lines the chest wall and the lungs.

portal vein — the large vein that carries blood from the abdominal digestive organs and spleen to the liver.

pseudopod — a temporary projection of the cytoplasm of a cell.

pus — fluid formed of lymph, dead cells, and live and dead bacteria when the body fights infection.

reflex — an involuntary response to a stimulus. Sneezing and coughing are reflexes.

spleen — an organ in the abdominal cavity, below the diaphragm and on the left side. It filters blood and eliminates aging cells.

systole — contractile period of the heart, when blood is pumped out into the arteries.

trachea — the air passage between the larynx and the primary bronchi; windpipe.

urethra — the tube that carries urine from the bladder to outside the body.

vasoconstriction — contraction of a blood vessel, usually due to injury or a drop in temperature.

veins — vessels that carry blood, usually low in oxygen, toward the heart; the smallest are venules.

vena cavae — the two large veins that carry blood to the right atrium of the heart.

ventricle — one of two muscular lower chambers of the heart that pump blood through the body.

More Books to Read

Blood. Steve Parker (Millbrook Press)

Blood Circulation. Andres Ruiz (Sterling)

The Body. Young Scientist Concepts and Projects (series). Steve Parker (Gareth Stevens)

The Circulatory System. Regina Avraham (Chelsea House)

The Heart. Seymour Simon (Morrow Junior Books)

Heart and Blood. Jan Burges (Silver Burdett Press)

Lungs and Breathing. Mark Lambert (Silver Burdett Press)

Our Bodies. Under the Microscope (series). Casey Horton (Gareth Stevens)

The Respiratory System. Jenny Bryan (Silver Burdett Press)

The Respiratory System. Mary Kittredge (Chelsea House)

Videos to Watch

Blood. (United Learning)

Breath of Life. (Films for the Humanities and Sciences)

Breath of Life: Our Respiratory System. (Rainbow Educational Media)

I Am Joe's Heart. (Pyramid Media)

I Am Joe's Lung. (Pyramid Media)

Microbeasts and Disease. Scientific Eye (series). (Journal Films and Video)

Web Sites to Visit

www.innerbody.com/tutorial2/tutorial.html   www.vis.colostate.edu/cgi-bin/gva/gvaview

www.cellsalive.com/antibody.htm   johns.largnet.uwo.ca/shine/health/body.htm

Some web sites stay current longer than others. For further web sites, use your browsers to locate the following topics: *anatomy, biology, blood, circulation, heart, human body, lungs, physiology,* and *respiration.*

Index